Tom Jackson

Raintree is an imprint of Capstone Global Library Limited, a company incorporated in
England and Wales having its registered office at 7 Pilgrim Street, London EC4V 6LB
Registered company number 6695582

www.raintree.co.uk
myorders@raintree.co.uk

ISBN: 978-1-4747-0235-5 (HB)
ISBN: 978-1-4747-0241-6

For Brown Bear Books Ltd:
Text: Tom Jackson
Designer: Lynne Lennon
Design Manager: Keith Davis
Editorial Director: Lindsey Lowe
Children's Publisher: Anne O'Daly
Picture Manager: Sophie Mortimer
Production Director: Alastair Gourlay

British Library Cataloguing in Publication Data
A full catalogue record for this book is available from the British Library.

**Acknowledgements**
t=top, c=centre, b=bottom, l=left, r=right
Front cover: Suzi Esterhas/Minden/FLPA
1, Jonas Gratzer/Lightrocket/Getty Images; 4, James Michael Dorsey/Shutterstock; 5t, Paulsly/Shutterstock; 5b, AndreAnita/
Shutterstock; 6, Filipe Frazao/Shutterstock; 7, Heiko Kiera/Shutterstock; 8, Czesznak Zsolt/Shutterstock; 9t, visceralimage/
Shutterstock; 9b, Dave Pusey/Shutterstock; 10, Annetje/Shutterstock; 11t, Zoonar/Thinkstock; 11b, Pavel L Photo and Video/
Shutterstock; 12, Wild Wonders Europe/Widstr/Nature PL; 13t, Alta Oosthuizen/Shutterstock; 13b, Ammit/iStock/Thinkstock;
14, Ewan Chesser/Shutterstock; 15t, Jonathan Blair/Corbis; 15b, Jonas Gratzer/Lightrocket/Getty Images; 16, Wild Wonders
Europe/Widstr/Nature PL; 17, Koo/Shutterstock; 18, Jonas Gratzer/Lightrocket/Getty Images; 19, Wikipedia; 20, Greg
Marshall/National Geographic Creative; 21, Netfalls - Remy Musser/Shutterstock; 22t, Michael Nichols/National Geographic
Society/Corbis; 22b, Sean Nel/Dreamstime; 23t, Noam Wind/Shutterstock; 24, Pascal Goetgheluck/SPL; 25, Steve Winter/
National Geographic Creative; 26c, Ralph White/Corbis; 26b, Tanja Rosso/Dreamstime; 27t, JoeBreuer/Shutterstock; 28, Sam
Ogden/SPL; 29, PA Images.

t=top, c=centre, b=bottom, l=left, r=right

Some words are shown in bold, **like this**. You can find out
what they mean by looking at the glossary.

Printed in China
20 19 18 17 16
10 9 8 7 6 5 4 3 2 1

# CONTENTS

# WHY WE TRACK ANIMAL BEHAVIOUR

Biologists are scientists. They study how animals live. To understand animals, biologists study behaviour in the wild. Sometimes they use technology to help them see behaviours that would otherwise be hidden from view.

## TYPES OF BEHAVIOUR

Animals live in many different ways, but they are all trying to do the same kinds of things. These things include finding food, finding mates and producing young. All animals also need to keep themselves and their young safe from attack by other animals.

This grey whale is "spyhopping". While **migrating**, the whale pokes its head out of the water. It can see land in the distance, and that helps it find its way.

A male and female lion are fighting. Animals fight over food, mates and **territory**.

Scientists call these activities animal behaviour. Biologists study how different species of animal do these things.

## NATURAL CONDITIONS

Animals change their behaviour depending on events. For example, if a gazelle is grazing and it detects a lion, it will stop eating and run away. Animals usually change their behaviour when they see humans, too. This makes it hard for scientists to be sure they are watching natural behaviour. Technology is used to help scientists track animal behaviour without being spotted.

## HIDDEN BEHAVIOUR

Technology can also be used to record animal behaviour when scientists are not there. It can show what animals are doing in places humans cannot go, such as in burrows under the ground or in the deep oceans. From studying behaviour, scientists can understand how animals survive.

These two crowned cranes are performing a **courtship ritual**. Their behaviour creates a bond between them. The cranes will mate every year to produce chicks.

5

# MAKING OBSERVATIONS

The easiest way to study animal behaviour is to simply watch animals in the wild. Biologists might spend hours outside watching what the animals do. Scientists also use binoculars and cameras so they can observe behaviour in detail.

## CHANGING CONDITIONS

An animal's behaviour changes throughout the day and night. Biologists have to observe behaviour to understand animals properly. A species' behaviour may also change with the seasons. For example, many animals breed only at a particular time of year.

A birdwatcher uses binoculars to look at birds flying over a wetland. Watching animals at a distance helps to create a picture of their natural behaviour.

A baby python hatches from its egg. By observing it, scientists know that the snake cuts its way out of the egg with an eggtooth. This is a pointed horn on the snout that falls off as soon as the head is out of the egg.

## USING SCIENCE

Biologists can often better understand behaviour by watching and describing what an animal does. They can learn about courtship rituals, which are the behaviours male and female animals perform before they mate. However, scientists must not assume they know what an animal's behaviour means without testing their idea scientifically. People used to think that all male bullfrogs croak to attract mates. This belief changed when scientists noticed that some bullfrogs stay silent. These silent bullfrogs mate with the females that come looking for the croaking males.

## OBSERVATION TECHNIQUES

Scientists observe animal behaviour with the naked eye while sitting quietly among the animals. They also watch from a distance, using a telescope or binoculars. Observations can also be made using cameras that take photographs and videos. Cameras can be set up to do this automatically without the researcher being there.

# HIDING OUT

Getting a good look at animals behaving naturally in the wild is not easy. Most animals are shy and will try to keep away from humans. Scientists have developed ways of staying out of sight.

## TAKING COVER

Many animals are camouflaged. This means their fur or skin is patterned to help them blend in with their surroundings. The camouflage makes it harder to see the animals. Wildlife experts copy this idea.

Wildlife experts watch animals from inside well-camouflaged hides. Even the big lenses of their cameras are disguised.

When observing animals, scientists do not wear brightly coloured clothes. Instead, they wear clothes that blend in with their surroundings. Sometimes, scientists dress in full camouflage gear like soldiers wear. To hide completely, scientists sit inside camouflaged shelters, or hides. An animal does not see the person or people inside.

A wildlife researcher is wearing clothes that keep him well hidden in the dry grass.

## OTHER SENSES

Wild animals use their senses of smell and hearing to detect danger. Scientists must be very quiet. Even the slightest sound can scare animals away. Scientists also use the wind to stay hidden. They choose a hiding place where the wind direction will blow their **odour** away from animals, not towards them. If an animal detects the smell of humans, it will run away.

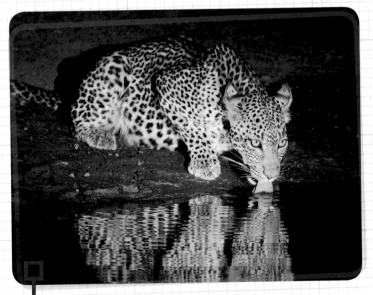

A night-vision camera makes it possible to see a leopard drinking at a watering hole at night.

### WOW!

Nocturnal animals use the cover of darkness to stay hidden. Night-vision equipment makes it easier for researchers to watch them. This equipment works by picking up the heat given off by the animals' bodies. Human eyes cannot see heat, but the night-vision equipment converts the heat into an image that can be seen.

# PICTURES AND VIDEOS

Cameras are useful tools for tracking animal behaviour. Many behaviours happen too fast for scientists to see them clearly. Looking at videos and photographs allows scientists to study what happens in much more detail.

## TOO MUCH, TOO FAST

The behaviour of animals that live in groups is complicated. Different animals in the group do different things, and they all do them at the same time. To understand the behaviour, scientists study photographs or **slow-motion** video.

For example, a school (group) of fish appears to change direction at the same time. It is almost as if the school was one single animal.

This diver is using an underwater camera. The bright light held above the camera makes it easier to see animals in the dark water.

However, video footage shows that fish on the outside of the school try to swim into the middle. The fish in the middle are too crowded and swim out. The result is the fish always stay in a tight ball, even when the group changes direction.

## HIDDEN DETAILS

Cameras can also show how small animals behave. The camera can magnify the animals. Magnified photographs show scientists how bugs feed, hunt and breed.

A close-up view shows a crab spider attacking a bee landing on a flower.

## TECHNOLOGY: Crane camera

A crane camera is a simple system for showing researchers large groups of animals. The camera is raised high above the ground on the arm of a crane. A wire connects the camera to scientists on the ground. They can see what the camera sees from high above the animals.

# Vulture watchpoints

Vultures are nature's rubbish disposal units. The big birds eat what is left of dead animals. Wildlife enthusiasts use hides to watch the birds in action.

**S**cientists and wildlife enthusiasts take advantage of vulture behaviour to get a good look at the birds. They build hidden watchpoints and then lure the birds to them with food.

## Soaring in the sky

Vultures are **scavengers**. They eat the bodies of dead animals. The birds look for animals that have died from old age, or they eat the remains of a meal left by a predator. To find food, vultures soar high above the ground. From this height they can see or smell bodies lying on the ground. The birds then circle down to rip off chunks of meat with their tough, hooked beaks. In dry areas and mountains, where vultures are common, it is normal to see the birds in the sky. However, to watch them on the ground is more difficult. That is why scientists build watchpoints.

### Watchpoint

A vulture watchpoint is a high-tech hide. It has mirrored windows. The people inside can see out, but the animals outside cannot see in. The experts inside poke their camera lenses out through curtains under the windows.

## Feeding behaviour

Scientists use watchpoints to observe vulture behaviour. This includes finding out which body parts the birds eat and how they interact with other scavengers, such as **jackals**.

### Bearded vulture

This African vulture eats bones. It carries a big bone in its claws high into the air. The bird then drops the bone on rocks below. The bone smashes into chunks that are small enough to swallow.

### King vulture

This species from Central and South America is one of the largest vultures in the world. Its wings are 2 metres (6.6 feet) wide. It soars over mountains, grasslands, and rainforest looking for food.

Scientists use hilltop watchpoints to watch the vultures in the air or resting on cliffs.

Vultures soar on currents of warm air that rise up from the ground.

Fresh meat and bones are placed in front of the hide to attract birds.

The ground watchpoint is accessed by a tunnel so the birds are not disturbed.

# REMOTE SENSING

Scientists cannot watch everything an animal does. Instead, researchers use technology to track animals 24 hours a day. This type of technology is called **remote** sensing.

## SEE IT ALL

Animals have a wide range of behaviours. They may only exhibit some of them once a day or even once a year. Scientists are not able to watch all the time. Remote sensing enables scientists to observe every moment of an animal's behaviour.

This elephant has a radio tracker attached to a collar around her neck. The tracker shows scientists where the elephant and her herd go day and night.

## TECHNOLOGY: Reusing radar

**Radar** technology was designed for tracking aircraft. It is also used by weather **satellites** to scan for rain. The same radar systems can be used to track animals. This radar scan shows a flock of 2 million birds flying near an airport in the American state of South Carolina. Scientists are investigating what made all these birds group together.

## TRACKING MOVEMENTS

Trackers are one form of remote sensing technology. These are small devices fitted to animals. They send out signals that tell scientists where the animal is. Trackers help researchers to work out what an animal does at different times of the day. For example, trackers show when an animal is drinking or feeding and where it goes to have a rest.

## KEEPING WATCH

Remote-sensing equipment is also used to take pictures and videos of animals in the wild. This technology is sometimes called a camera trap. It does not trap the animal itself but takes a picture of it. Camera traps are used to study animals that are very rare or difficult to find in their natural **habitat**.

A scientist fits a **trail camera** to a rainforest tree. He will then leave the area so he does not scare away the animals.

# WEBCAMS

A webcam is a camera that is connected to the Internet. Any photographs or video taken by the camera are sent to a website. Webcams are a good way of watching how animals behave in nests and dens.

A webcam records the behaviour of a whiskered tern as it sits on its nest in marshland. This bird lives in Europe, Asia and Africa.

## INTERNET VIDEO

A wildlife webcam uses the same kind of camera as a mobile phone or computer screen. However, a webcam is left outside for a long time and needs a tough, waterproof case. Video is sent to the Internet using the same kind of system as videophone programs.

The camera is operated by remote control. It may be turned off at night when it is too dark to take video. Where there is no electricity supply, the camera equipment is powered by batteries or a small **solar panel**. The camera is connected to the Internet by a cable or by a **wireless** link.

## ONE LOCATION

Webcams are best for watching nests, dens and other places where animals return every day (or night). The cameras give a close-up view of the animals resting in the den. In the breeding season, scientists can watch the animals raising young.

## JOIN IN

### watching wildlife

There are many wildlife webcams you can watch on the web. Some show live video of animals, while others show examples of interesting behaviour. Search online for wildlife webcams. Try these organisations first:

**The Wildlife Trusts**
**Explore.org**

There are webcams for eagles and other birds of prey, burrowing animals such as badgers and even for bears.

These badgers are leaving their den, or sett, at dusk. "Settcams" show how the badgers behave as they spend the day underground.

**FACT**: Falcons nest on tall buildings, and some wildlife webcams are on the top of skyscrapers.

# VIDEO TRAPS

Video traps are used to record the behaviour of animals that range over wide areas. These cameras often record very rare behaviour that scientists have never observed.

## HEAT SENSOR

The cameras used in video traps do not take pictures all the time. To save battery power, they switch on only when an animal moves in front of them. Each camera is fitted with a heat-sensitive detector. When the camera detects the body heat of an animal, the camera starts filming a video.

Scientists watch a rare Sumatran tiger captured on video by cameras set up in the rainforest.

## RARE BEHAVIOUR

Video traps allow scientists to watch the behaviour of shy animals. Animals, such as tigers and giant pandas, are cautious. Anything unusual stops them from behaving naturally. Video traps have been used to watch both species. Video has also shown that when two pandas meet, they roar to scare each other away. If that does not work, the pandas fight, biting and slashing each other with their claws. The fighting is so violent that the pandas knock down young trees. Video traps show where tigers go when they are resting during the day – they hunt at night. Videos have also shown female tigers playing with their cubs. Few scientists have ever seen this behaviour in the wild.

A self-portrait taken by a crested black macaque.

### WOW!

In 2011, a wildlife photographer on the island of Sulawesi in Indonesia was taking pictures of crested black macaques, a rare type of monkey. One of the monkeys picked up a camera and started to take pictures – even grinning at the lens.

This monkey species is in danger of **extinction**. There are just 6,000 left in the wild.

# CREATURE CAM

One of the best ways to understand how an animal behaves is to attach a camera to it. This special camera is nicknamed a "creature cam". Creature cam videos show scientists what an animal is seeing.

A penguin fitted with a creature cam is sliding into a hole in the ice. The camera gives the penguin's view of its hunt for fish to eat.

## BODY CAMERA

Creature cams are designed not to bother the animals wearing them. They can only be fitted to animals large enough to carry one without the camera changing their natural behaviour. Creature cams are often placed on the back of swimming animals, such as sea turtles and sharks.

Creature cams give a close-up view of the behaviour of dangerous animals, such as alligators and crocodiles.

The camera does not weigh very much in water, so it does not create problems for the animal. Smaller, lighter cameras have been developed. These can be fitted to land animals, such as lions.

## TAKING VIDEO

Creature cams are attached in a number of ways. A shark's camera is clamped to its fin. A penguin or seal is fitted with a special harness. A dolphin or whale has one attached with strong suckers that stick to the animal's smooth skin.

The first creature cams had small batteries and could take only a few minutes of video. To watch the video, scientists had to catch the animal and remove the camera. The latest cameras are designed to detach by remote control. Scientists collect the cameras and download the video.

## JOIN IN

### Creature cams online

The amazing videos from creature cams are available online. Search online for this organisation and look for the links to the creature cam videos:

**National Geographic**

There are videos of alligators, penguins, sea lions, whales, bull sharks, lions, sea turtles and even a tree kangaroo. Many of the videos show the animals hunting prey.

# Lion hunt

Creature cams and night-vision equipment have allowed scientists to study a lion hunt in more detail than ever before.

Lions are the only cats that work together to hunt prey. A group of lions is called a pride. Prides hunt at night. Researchers use the latest night-vision technology to watch how they do it.

## Hunting ground

Most lions live in the grasslands of Africa. They share this habitat with **antelopes**. For safety, antelopes live in herds. They eat grasses and leaves. They are very fast runners and can outrun a lion. Antelopes are the lions' main food. To catch one, the lions have to work as a team.

Researchers record lion hunts with a creature cam around a **lioness's** neck. However, scientists normally use special night-vision equipment to see how all the lions behave during hunts.

### Night vision

Researchers stay out of sight when watching lions. They use red lights to help them see in the dark. Lions cannot see that colour very well. However, lions can see clearly at night. Their eyes have a mirror-like layer. This reflects the dim light back into the eye so it has enough light to see.

## Eating order

Only the lionesses take part in the hunt. The pride's male lion gets to eat the kill first. Then the adult females eat. Finally the cubs are allowed to have some food.

## In for the kill

The lionesses form the hunting team. The single male lion in the pride sits and watches with the cubs. The lionesses stay **downwind** of the antelope herd. That means the wind is blowing their odour away from their prey, so the prey cannot smell them. The pride stays out of sight until the lionesses are ready to launch an attack.

### Killer bite

A lioness kills her prey with a two-stage process. First the cat knocks her prey to the ground. Then the lioness bites the antelope's neck and crushes it with her powerful bite. That breaks the prey's neck and kills it.

**2** Some lionesses creep around behind the herd. They jump out and scare the antelopes.

**3** The herd runs away from the lionesses.

**1** Lionesses approach a herd of antelopes from downwind.

**4** One lioness waits for the herd to get close and grabs one of them.

# TRACKING WITH ROBOTS

Robots help scientists to study animal behaviour in two ways. First, robots are programmed to copy an animal behaviour so scientists can study it. Second, robots can operate in places that are too dangerous for humans.

A real ant meets a robot ant. The robot is designed to copy the way real ants explore an area.

## COPYING BEHAVIOUR

Robots are used to study ants. These insects live in **colonies** containing thousands of animals. Working together, the ants in a colony can do many things. For example, ant colonies build nests, find food and carry building materials and young over long distances.

Tiny robots are used to work out how ants behave. The robot is designed to move like an ant. It goes in a straight line until it cannot go any further. It then changes direction and goes forwards again. Scientists release many robots at the same time. They find that even these simple robots spread out and fill the whole area – just like real ants.

A young tiger investigates a camera robot sent by scientists to take pictures of its behaviour.

## DANGEROUS PLACES

Robots are sent to places that humans cannot reach. They can be sent to investigate caves, ice-covered seas and deep water. Robots are all controlled remotely by a human driver. The driver can see what the robot is doing on a computer screen.

**FACT:** BigDog, a four-legged robot, can run, climb hills and even throw objects.

# ROV submersibles

Humans cannot visit the animals on the deep sea floor. Robots and other machines are sent instead.

Most of the world's sea floor is more than 1.6 kilometres (1 mile) under the sea's surface. At that depth the weight of all the water above is enough to squash a human body flat. Most of the exploration is done by robots.

## Underwater

A submarine is a craft that carries people underwater. Submarines that can go all the way to the deep sea floor are very expensive. Scientists use ROV **submersibles** instead. ROV stands for "Remotely Operated underwater Vehicle".

ROVs can reach the deepest parts of the ocean. The ROV is connected to the surface by a long cable. The cable carries electrical power for the engines and steering commands from a human controller. It is always dark on the sea floor. ROVs are fitted with bright lights and cameras so the controller can see and study any animals the ROV might find.

### underwater robots

ROVs can be as big as a car or small enough for a person to pick up. They have at least two engines, or thrusters. ROVs are steered by making one thruster push harder than the others.

## Research ship

Scientists research the oceans while aboard special ships. They spend months at sea gathering information. These scientists are called oceanographers. They study ocean life, the weather and the motion of the water.

This ROV is in two parts. The lower one drops to the sea floor.

Several probes collect samples from the water and the sandy sea floor. Information is sent back to shore by satellite.

Depth sensors show the crew the shape of the sea floor.

## Studying the sea floor

The research ship takes many measurements and samples from the water and the sea floor. The ROV sends back pictures and can even capture animals to study. ROVs have detected many new forms of life living in the deepest parts of the ocean.

# THE FUTURE

There are many things that scientists do not know about animal behaviour. In the future, scientists will use robots that work like real creatures to work out why animals do the things they do. Drone aircraft will also watch behaviour in the wild.

## ROBOT ANIMALS

Robot **engineers** often copy animal bodies when they design robots. A robot moves like an animal and senses objects using the same systems. That means a robot can be used for investigating animal behaviour in the laboratory.

Robot tests in the future could tell scientists how much an animal thinks about what it is doing. The robot is programmed to follow simple rules. Scientists will run tests to see how well the robot performs tasks, such as moving around a maze.

RoboPike is a robot fish that can swim by itself. This version is remote controlled. Scientists are developing a robot that can find its way around by itself.

Scientists want to know if the robot does these things in the same way that animals would do them in the wild. If the robot does not behave like a natural animal, that shows scientists that their programmed rules do not match the way an animal makes its decisions. That could mean that animals are taking more things into account before making their next movement. However, if the robot does behave like a wild animal, it might show that animals do not need to think much at all. Even complicated animal behaviour, such as finding food and mates or getting away from predators, only requires the animal to perform a few automatic actions.

A park ranger launches a small drone aircraft to track tigers. In the future drones could be used to keep an eye on all kinds of wildlife.

## AUTOMATIC AIRCRAFT

Drones are another kind of robot. They are small uncrewed aircraft. They may become a useful tool in tracking behaviour. In the future drones could stay in the air for many days. They could carry powerful cameras to watch wildlife closely. Drone research will show how the behaviour of one animal can affect the behaviour of others over a wide area.

# GLOSSARY

**antelope** hoofed animal that has horns

**colony** large group of animals that live and work together

**courtship ritual** complex dance-like behaviour used by animals to attract mates

**downwind** located in a place where wind is blowing towards you; animals cannot smell things that are downwind

**engineer** person who uses the latest scientific knowledge to build machines

**extinct** no longer existing

**habitat** place where animals or plants live and grow

**jackal** small dog that lives in Africa and Asia; jackals live in large packs and mostly eat the remains of dead animals

**lioness** female lion

**migrate** make a regular journey to find food, find mates or raise young

**nocturnal** active at night

**odour** smell

**radar** technology that bounces radio waves off objects and picks up any echoes that come back; the system is used to detect large objects that are too far away to see with the naked eye

**remote** a long distance away from anything else

**satellite** object that orbits (moves around) another larger one; planets are satellites of the Sun, and machines launched in orbit are also known as satellites

**scavenger** animal that eats the remains of dead animals

**slow-motion** video of real-life action that is slowed down so the fast motion can be seen in detail

**solar panel** technology that generates electricity from sunlight

**submersible** submarine that does not have a human crew

**territory** in biology, this is a region controlled by an animal; the animal finds all its food in the territory and tries to stop other members of its species from living there

**trail camera** tough camera that is designed to work outside in all weathers

**wireless** Internet connection that uses radio waves instead of wires